A Study Guide for

When You Can't Trust HIS Heart

Discovering the
Limitless Love of God

Marci Julin

A Study Guide for

When You Can't Trust HIS Heart

Discovering the
Limitless Love of God

Printed in the United States of America

ISBN-13: 978-1512063882

ISBN-10: 1512063886

Learn more information at:

www.HeartandMindMinistries.com

"He who is wise, let him consider the great love of the LORD."

Psalm 107:43

Dear Reader,

I've found the saying, "You get out of it what you put into it," to be true when encountering life-changing truth. I wrote <u>When You Can't Trust His Heart</u> as I meditated, studied, contemplated, prayed & discussed with others the abundant Scriptures on God's personal love. As a result, I have never been the same. I long for others who have been battered and bruised by life to have their thinking on God's love radically transformed by the renewing of their minds through God's powerful Holy Spirit and His Word. This takes time and focus.

I have not the slightest doubt that God desperately longs for His children to truly grasp and know His limitless love so that they might fully trust Him, but so few of His children do. My hope is that this guide enables you to begin to change that. This study guide can enable you individually or as a group to zero in and focus on the key concepts and Scriptures found in my book. And, don't forget to daily pray the Love Prayer because significant transformations only occur through the Holy Spirit's power. May you never be the same!

In Christ's awesome love,

Marci Julin ☺

Contents

Part 1: Struggle

Part 2: Power

Part 3: Love

Part 4: Trust

Part 1

Struggle

CHAPTER 1

A Devastating Thought

1. On a scale of 1-10, (with 1 being not at all) how would you rate the truth of the statement, "Life is hard."

   1 - 2 - 3 - 4 - 5 - 6 - 7 - 8 - 9 - 10

2. On a scale of 1-10, (with 1 being not at all) how anxious or fearful do you tend to be?

   1 - 2 - 3 - 4 - 5 - 6 - 7 - 8 - 9 - 10

Do you think your ratings in questions 1 and 2 might indicate that you need to trust God more?

3. Take a few minutes to jot down some of the key events in your life that cause you to struggle with believing God truly loves you as an individual and/or that cause you to struggle with trusting God.

   - _____
   - _____
   - _____

- _____
- _____
- _____
- _____

4. In the book, I give an analogy of a nervous neighbor walking home from the store compared to a little girl walking home with her daddy (p 2-4). Which one more closely compares to your relationship with God on a consistent basis? Why?

_____

_____

5. Comment on the following quote from the conclusion of chapter 1,

> *Perhaps, like me, you "trust" Him as long as He works things out to your liking, but then find yourself disillusioned when He does not. Is that really trust? Do you find it difficult to accept, as I did, that God truly loves you when He allows pain to enter your life?*

_____

_____

_____

6. I wrote about how the counselor challenged me to find Scriptures that spoke about God's love for me and to make the conscious decision to trust that those verses applied specifically to me. I now challenge you to do the same. If you're willing to accept that challenge, please take a moment to sign the challenge at the end of this chapter.

7. In the Old Testament we are told of how precious God's chosen people, the Jews, are to Him. In the New Testament Paul writes to the Galatians saying,

> *You are all sons of God through faith in Christ Jesus, for all of you who were baptized into Christ have clothed yourselves with Christ...If you belong to Christ, then you are Abraham's seed, and heirs according to the promise.* (3:26,27 & 29)

With those verses in mind, read **Psalm 102:13-17**. What picture does this portray of how God views the brokenness of His people? Does it offer you any encouragement?

_____

_____

_____

_____

Verses for Meditation:

> *When I said, 'My foot is slipping,' your love, O LORD, supported me. When anxiety was great within me, your consolation brought joy to my soul.*
> **(Psalm 94:18-19)**

There was hope for me, and there is hope for you!

My Trust Challenge

I, _____ choose, from this day forward, that I will consciously choose to trust God's Word when it speaks of His love for me and His pleasure in me as His child, whether I feel it or not.

_____
Signature

_____
Date

* For quick reference, use the lines below to record any meaningful Scripture references on God's love and His view of you that you discover during the course of this study.

_____

_____

_____

_____

_____

CHAPTER 2

Tools for the Journey

... to be made new in the attitude of your minds

(Ephesians 4:23)

1. How do you feel about Romans 8:28? Do you find comfort and encouragement from it during a trial? Why or why not?

   _____

   _____

   _____

2. Make a list of things in life that currently cause you moderate to severe stress.

   - _____
   - _____
   - _____
   - _____
   - _____

- _____
- _____
- _____
- _____
- _____

> *There is no fear in love. But perfect love casts out fear, because fear has to do with punishment. The man who fears is not made perfect in love.*
>
> (1 John 4:18)

3. Why does a lack of confidence in God's personal love result in fear?

_____

_____

_____

4. What are the two biblical tools available to every believer for repatterning one's thinking about God's love and trust?

- _____

- _____

5. The biblical tool of meditating on God's Word is *to silence and still oneself so that the mind can be filled with God's truth* (p 24). How could you incorporate this tool into your daily life in order to change the thoughts that determine your emotional and spiritual health?

_____

_____

_____

6. Since meditation begins by focusing on being filled with God's truth, consider and comment on what the following verses say about how God views you, and the hope He offers you.

- Isaiah 30:18

_____

_____

_____

- Isaiah 61:1-3

_____

_____

_____

7. Go back to your list in question 2. Circle any of the items in your list that God cannot lovingly handle.

8. Write a prayer to God that expresses in your own words your desire to trust Him and His love for you.

_____

_____

_____

_____

_____

_____

Verses for Meditation:

May your unfailing love come to me, O LORD...The earth is filled with your love, O LORD, teach me your decrees...May your unfailing love be my comfort, according to your promise to your servant. (Psalm 119:41,64&76))

CHAPTER 3

Introducing a
Transforming Prayer

For this reason I kneel before the Father

(Ephesians 3:14)

1. Read the apostle Paul's introduction to the Love Prayer in **Ephesians 3:1-15**. Is there anything in particular that jumps out at you?

_____

_____

_____

2. What is the *mystery* that Paul refers to in verses 4-6?

_____

_____

_____

3. Why does Paul consider the privilege of direct access to God, mentioned in verse 11, to be one of the riches of God? What does that privilege mean to you?

_____

_____

_____

_____

4. Read **Hebrews 10:19-23**.

   Why can one enter God's presence with confidence?

_____

_____

_____

5. Why does Paul view the privilege of complete access to God as a cause for encouragement, when it did not bring relief from his problems? (p 41).

_____

_____

_____

_____

6. Why does Paul kneeling to offer the Love Prayer on our behalf signify just how crucial it is for believers to truly know the love of God?

_____

_____

_____

Verses for Meditation:

...the LORD has compassion on those who fear him, for he knows how we are formed, he remembers that we are dust. As for man, his days are like grass...But from everlasting the LORD's love is with those who fear him.
Psalm 146:13-17

The Love Prayer

I pray that out of his glorious riches he may strengthen you with power through his Spirit in your inner being, so that Christ may dwell in your hearts through faith.

And I pray that you, being rooted and established in love, may have power, together with all the saints, to grasp how wide and long and high and deep is the love of Christ, and to know this love that surpasses knowledge-- that you may be filled to the measure of all the fullness of God.

Now to him who is able to do immeasurably more than all we ask or imagine, according to his power that is at work within us, to him be glory in the church and in Christ Jesus throughout all generations, forever and ever! Amen.

Ephesians 3:16-21

Part 2

Power

CHAPTER 4

Inward Power

I pray that out of his glorious riches he may strengthen you with power through his Spirit in your inner being (vs. 16).

1. The Love Prayer begins with a request for inner strengthening. How have you experienced weakness in your life? What sort of emotions did/does weakness arouse in you?

   _____

   _____

   _____

2. God offers His children *glorious riches*. In the last chapter we discussed one of those riches--the privilege of direct access to God through Jesus Christ. In this chapter we learn of another rich blessing of God--strength through the Holy Spirit. Read the verses in the box on the next page.

> *Because you are sons, God sent the Spirit of his Son into our hearts, the Spirit who calls out, "Abba, Father."* (Galatians 4:6)
>
> _____
>
> *Peter replied, "Repent and be baptized, every one of you, in the name of Jesus Christ so that your sins may be forgiven. And you will receive the gift of the Holy Spirit."* (Acts 2:38)

According to those verses, how and when does an individual receive the gift of the Holy Spirit?

_____

_____

_____

3. Why are *spiritual strength* and *power* prerequisites for truly knowing the love of God?

_____

_____

4. What Greek word does Paul use for power three times in the Love Prayer?

_____

5. Paul describes the type of power that we should pray for in **Ephesians 1:19-20** in order to grasp the love of God.

> *...and his incomparably great power for us who believe. That power is like the working of his mighty strength, which he exerted in Christ when he raised him from the dead and seated him at his right hand in the heavenly realm.*

What type of power is this?

_____

6. The inner strengthening through the Holy Spirit's power is needed in our *inner being*. The only other time in the Bible that the *inner being* is referred to is found in **2 Corinthians 4:16**.

> *For which cause we faint not; but though our outward man perish, yet the inward man is renewed day by day* (KJV).

Is the inner man physical of spiritual? What is this inner man and why is it important?

_____

_____

_____

Why do we need to be *renewed day by day* through the Holy Spirit's power?

_____

_____

Verses for Meditation:

> *But I will sing of your strength; in the morning I will sing of your love, for you are my fortress in times of trouble. O my Strength, I sing praise to you; you, O God, are my fortress, my loving God. (Psalm 59:6-7)*

CHAPTER 5

The Difficulty With Trust

I pray that out of his glorious riches he may strengthen you with power through his Spirit in your inner being so that Christ may dwell in your hearts through faith. (vs. 16-17a)

1. What is the purpose stated in Ephesians 3:16-17 behind the request that you be strengthened with power in your inner being?

    _____

    _____

2. The word *dwell* used in this verse means... (p 65)

    _____

3. A pet requires adequate food, shelter, and care for hospitable dwelling. In a spiritual sense, how do you make your heart a welcome home to Christ?

_____

4. Faith and _____ (a biblical synonym for faith) are commanded and mentioned over 235 times in the Bible. Why do you think trusting God is so important to Him?

_____

_____

Whoever trusts in the LORD, happy is he. *(Proverbs 16:20 NKJ).*

5. Why do you think that someone would be happy who trusts in the LORD? Apply this to your own life.

_____

_____

_____

6. Read Psalm 16:5-11. List all of the phrases from these verses that describe a closeness with the LORD.

  * _____

  * _____

  * _____

  * _____

7. The last half of chapter 5 offers numerous biblical proofs that God understands the struggle to trust Him. What can you do to overcome this struggle?

_____

_____

Verse for Meditation:

But I trust in your unfailing love; my heart rejoices in your salvation..
Psalm 13:5

Part 3

Love

CHAPTER 6

Understanding Your Roots

And I pray that you, being rooted and established in love, (v.17b)

1.   According to chapter 6, where were Christians rooted and established in love?

2. Why does the story of Jesus' suffering and death on the cross communicate love to you--be specific?

3. According to **John 3:16** and other verses, Jesus died for the sins of the whole world. However, according to **John 1:12** how does one actually make use of the cross and become a child of God?

> *Yet to all who did receive him, to those who believed in his name, he gave the right to become children of God— children born not of natural descent, nor of human decision or a husband's will, but born of God.*
>
> **(John 1:12)**

_____

_____

_____

4. This chapter focuses on the gruesome details of Christ's suffering on the cross, which is unpleasant to consider. **Read 1 Corinthians 11:23-29**. Why does God command that we remember <u>both</u> the body and the blood of our Lord?

_____

_____

_____

5. What does chapter 6 suggest is the meaning of the metaphor of our being *rooted and established in love*? (p90)

_____

_____

6. In summary, by no means is the cross the final demonstration of God's love for you, but it is the starting point. Have you made the decision to believe in and accept this incredible demonstration of God's love for you? If not, there is no time like the present. Is there anything keeping you from trusting Jesus as your Savior right now?

_____

Verse for Meditation:

> *See what great love the Father has lavished on us, that we should be called the children of God! And that is what we are!*
>
> *(1 John 3:1)*

CHAPTER 7

Just As I Am

How much more, then, will the blood of Christ... cleanse our consciences from acts that lead to death, so that we may serve the living God!
(Hebrews 9:14)

1. On a scale of 1-10, (with 1 being not at all pleased and 10 being perfectly pleased) how would you rate how pleased you *feel* God is with you (be honest)?

   1 - 2 - 3 - 4 - 5 - 6 - 7 - 8 - 9 - 10

2. Where does that perception of how God views you come from?

   _____

   _____

3. **1 John 4:8** says, *God is love*. Therefore, God defines love and a description of true love would be a description of God. With that in mind, read the following passages to look for indications as to whether or not God's love is unconditional.

- **1 Corinthians 13:4-7**
- **1 John 4:18**
- **Romans 5:8**

What would you conclude about God's love for you from these verses?

_____

_____

_____

4. Why did Jesus NOT condemn the woman caught in adultery (**John 8:1-11**)?

_____

_____

5. How is it possible for a holy God to NOT judge, condemn, and punish our sin? **Read 2 Corinthians 5:21 and Romans 3:23-26**.

_____

_____

> *He who conceals his sins does not prosper, but whoever confesses and renounces them finds mercy.* (Proverbs 28:13)

6. According to this verse and **1 John 1:9**, what is the correct way to deal with sin, and what is the end result?

_____

_____

7. Read **1 Corinthians 6:9-11.** Everyone has a past, but as verse 11 says, **And that is what some of you WERE. BUT you were washed, you were sanctified, you were justified in the name of the Lord Jesus and by the Spirit of our God.** Is there any sin that doesn't fall within the list of sins that can be forgiven? Apply this to yourself.

_____

8. Other reasons besides sin can cause you to think that God is displeased with you, such as things you perceive as personality flaws, lack of talent, events of life, education, accomplishments, etc. Take a moment to consider if any such reasons are interfering with your ability to accept God's unconditional love for you.

_____

_____

_____

9. Write down the words to the verse from *Just As I Am* that speaks the most to you.

_____

_____

_____

Will you make the following verse from Charlotte Elliot's hymn, *Just As I Am* your concluding prayer today?

Just as I am, Thy love unknown

Hath broken every barrier down;

Now, to be Thine, yea, Thine alone,

O Lamb of God, I come, I come.

Verse for Meditation:

Though your sins are like scarlet, they shall be as white as snow; though they are red as crimson, they shall be like wool.

(Isaiah 1:18)

CHAPTER 8

The Necessity of the Body

And I pray that you, being rooted and established in love, may have power, together with all the saints, to grasp how wide and long and high and deep is the love of Christ (v17b-18)

1. Has there ever been a time when you experienced the Body of Christ reaching out to you with God's love? If so, describe it, and the affect it had on you?

   _____

   _____

   _____

2. Has there ever been a time when you were rejected or mistreated by the Body of Christ? If so, how did that affect you?

   _____

   _____

   _____

> *Unto the church of God which is at Corinth, to them that are sanctified in Christ Jesus, called to be saints, with all that in every place call upon the name of Jesus Christ our Lord, both their's and our's:*
> **1 Corinthians 1:2 (KJV)**

3. According to the above verse, who is a saint?

    _____

4. Read **1 John 4:7-21**. Why should God's people show love to others? What does it say about an individual if they do not?

    _____

    _____

> *Dear children, let us not love with words or tongue but with actions and in truth.* **1 John 3:18**

5. Why is loving primarily with actions rather than words so important?

    _____

    _____

    _____

6. The end of chapter 8 makes several challenges with action steps. Which of the following, if any, do you need to do?

☐ Find and get involved in a good church.

☐ Actively seek out ways to show God's love to others IN the Body of Christ.

☐ Allow those in the Body to minister His love to you.

Write specific actions you can take.

_____

_____

_____

Verses for Meditation:

> *Follow God's example, therefore, as dearly loved children and walk in the way of love, just as Christ loved us and gave himself up for us as a fragrant offering and sacrifice to God. (Ephesians 5:1-2)*

CHAPTER 9

The Limitless Love of Christ for You

---

may have power, together with all the saints, to grasp how wide and long and high and deep is the love of Christ, (vs. 18)

1. Read Job 11:7-9. Why does Paul enumerate the four dimensions of the love of Christ in the Love Prayer just like the author of Job did?

   _____

   _____

2. God's character dictates His behavior.

   - 1 John 4:16 says, *God is* _____.

   - Psalm 139:7-12 speaks of God's inescapable_____.

   - John 1:1-3 & Revelation 21:6 speak of the triune God being the Alpha & Omega, the _____ and the _____.

If God's character dictates that He must always act out of love, then the fact that He is omnipresent tells us that God's love is limitless.

3. With these truths in mind, why can you *flourish* by fully trusting in God's unfailing, limitless love?

> *But I am like an olive tree flourishing in the house of God; I trust in God's unfailing love forever and ever.* **Psalm 52:8**

_____

_____

_____

4. Why must love allow for free-will?

_____

_____

_____

_____

5. Everything, including all pain and suffering, fall under the sovereignty of God but are the result of the sin-cursed earth we live on. In this chapter three specific reasons for pain and suffering are given.

1. Acts of God such as natural disasters or physical infirmities

2. Sinful choices & actions of others

3. Our own sinful choices & actions

Make a personal list of pain and suffering in your own life that trouble you. Then think through and label the general reason for each item listed with the above #'s 1, 2 or 3.

☐ _____

☐ _____

☐ _____

☐ _____

☐ _____

☐ _____

☐ _____

Are there any people you need to forgive, including yourself?

_____

_____

6. Read **Psalm 136**. Use the format of that Psalm and the example of Marci's from this chapter (p137-139) to write your own personal Psalm that tells of God's loving gifts to you throughout your life. (If doing this as a group study, make this *homework* for the coming week.)

_____

_____

_____

_____

_____

_____

_____

_____

_____

_____

_____

_____

_____

_____

_____

_____

_____

_____

_____

_____

_____

_____

_____

_____

_____

_____

Verse for Meditation:

> *Let them give thanks to the Lord for his unfailing love and his wonderful deeds for mankind.* **Psalm 107:21**

CHAPTER 10

Grasping & Knowing Christ's Love for You

to grasp how wide and long and high and deep is the love of Christ,

and to know this love that surpasses knowledge (vs.18b-19)

1. What illustration does Marci give for understanding the Greek meaning of the verb *grasp* in verse 18--that we would *eagerly seize or possess an understanding of God's love for ourselves*?

_____

_____

2. The second verb, *know*, in verse 19 means...

_____

3. **Think of a relationship in which you are loved.** How do you know that this individual loves you?

_____

_____

Do you always behave in ways towards that individual that are deserving of **love**?

_____

Do you ever question that individual's **love** for you? Why?

_____

_____

When you *feel* **loved**, how do you behave in response?

_____

_____

4. Does the truth of God's love for you depend on whether or not you understand it or

feel it? _____ However, *until you _____ that love for yourself, you*

will not experience it as God intends (p149).

5. Read **Song of Songs 2:4-6/ 6:2-3 & 9/ 8:10-12**. Although this book of the Bible might make you blush, it is believed by scholars to be a picture of Christ's love for the church. In reading the verses above do you get the sense that this is a description of the mere intellectual ponderings of love? _____

If this is a picture of God's love for you, what stands out to you from those verses?

_____

_____

_____

6. In summary, what are the two action words that Paul prays for in verses 18 & 19 of the Love Prayer?

_____ & _____

Verse for Meditation:

But my dove, my perfect one, is unique...
(Song of Songs 6:9)

Part 4

Trust

CHAPTER 11

Fill'er Up!

that you may be filled to the measure of all the

fullness of God. (vs. 19b)

1. What is the illustration Marci gives of being *filled to the measure of all the fullness of God?*

   _____

   _____

2. What are the two Bible stories retold in this chapter that use the same Greek word for *fullness* that Ephesians 3:19 uses?

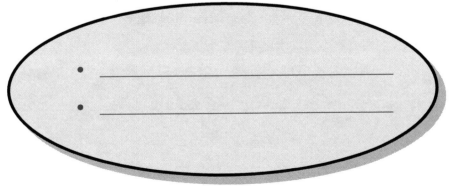

What is the literal meaning of the **root word** for both ***filled*** and ***fullness***?

_____

3. What is the literal meaning of ***fullness*** as used in verse 19?

_____

4. Take the time to read the two Bible stories referred to in the chapter:
   • **Matthew 14:13-21**

   ➡ In this story, what was the state of the people's stomachs?

   _____

   ➡ How do we know they had their fill after Jesus fed them?

   _____

   • **John 2:1-11**

What was the state of the wine jugs before they were filled to fullness with Jesus' good wine?

_____

Similarly, this chapter speaks of the need for believers to be emptied before God can fill them. Is there anything that God is calling to your mind that you need to be emptied of?

_____

_____

_____

> *Let my eyes overflow with tears night and day without ceasing; for my virgin daughter-- my people-- has suffered a grievous wound, a crushing blow.* **Jeremiah 14:17**

5. Jeremiah 14:17 speaks of how God feels about the wounds of His people. Rewrite it more specifically in your own words, as though God were speaking it to you.

_____

_____

_____

Can you do as David recommends in Psalm 62:8 *Pour out your hearts to him, for God is our refuge*. Write a prayer to God on the lines that follow doing just that.

_____

_____

_____

_____

_____

_____

_____

_____

_____

_____

_____

_____

_____

_____

_____

_____

_____

Verse for Meditation:

The grace of our Lord was poured out on me abundantly, along with the faith and love that are in Christ Jesus. (1 Timothy 1:14)

CHAPTER 12

Above & Beyond

Now to him who is able to do immeasurably more than all we ask or imagine, according to his power that is at work within us, to him be glory in the church and in Christ Jesus throughout all generations, forever and ever! Amen" (v. 20-21).

1. What are the superlatives that your version of the Bible uses in Ephesians 3:20?

_____

_____

2. How can God accomplish *more than all* you *ask or imagine* in you?

_____

3. Read Judges 6:1-16. Why could God call Gideon a *mighty warrior* when he was clearly a timid farmer?

_____

_____

> **But we have this treasure in jars of clay to show that this all surpassing power is from God and not from us. 1 Corinthians 4:7**

4. What does 1 Corinthians 4:7 mean when it refers to *jars of clay*?

_____

_____

According to that verse, why do the weaknesses of our flesh showcase the power of God?

_____

_____

5. According to Ephesians 3:18 & 21, why is it important that we are a part of the church?

_____

_____

6. The Love Prayer ends with *to him be glory in the church and in Christ Jesus throughout all generations forever and ever.* What do those words indicate about God's plan for the church? Will His plan change?

_____

_____

Verse for Meditation:

The LORD delights in those who fear him, who put their hope in his unfailing love. Psalm 147:11

CHAPTER 13

An End of Fear

There is no fear in love. But perfect love drives out fear, because fear has to do with punishment. The man who fears is not made perfect in love.

(I John 4:18)

1. Do you find that when you have a prayer need you feel that God will listen and respond to someone else better than you? If so, why?

   _____

   _____

2. Read **Hebrews 10:19-23**. According to these verses, what are the 3 factors (v22) that give us confidence that God will hear our prayers?

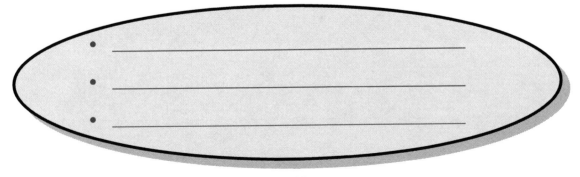

   - _____
   - _____
   - _____

3. Have you ever in your life experienced a time while suffering that stands out as a good memory in light of the love that was showed to you by someone(s)? (p 184-186)

_____

_____

> *There is no fear in love. But perfect love drives out fear, because fear has to do with punishment. The one who fears is not made perfect in love.*
> **1 John 4:18**

4. We are told to fear God in many places in the Bible (i.e. **1 Peter 2:17 / 2 Corinthians 5:11**), and yet in **1 John 4:18** we're told that perfect love drives out fear. The words used in both passages come from the root word *phobos* from which we get the word *phobia*. What kind of fear of God are we to have and what kind of fear are we NOT to have of God as His children?

_____

_____

_____

_____

5. Take the time to read all of **Romans 8**. Briefly list the main point of each section from this passage. The first one is done for you.

- vs 1-4: _Jesus met the requirements of the law and set us free_

- vs 5-11: _____

- vs 12-17: _____

- vs 18-25: _____

- vs 26-27 _____

- vs 28-34: _____

- vs 34-39-: _____

6. I would summarize the logic of Romans 8 in this way:

   Jesus' work at the cross gave us a new spirit that makes us children of God. Fear is contrary to that Spirit, but we can choose to walk according to the old nature. God allows His Son and the Holy Spirit to intercede for us, works always for our good, and nothing and no one can come in between us and God. Therefore, God's perfect love should cast out fear.

   In light of that, what applications can you make to your specific thoughts and actions?

   _____

   _____

   _____

   _____

Dear One,

Because of His deep love for you, God can be trusted. He gave us the Love Prayer because He understands that, humanly speaking, such trust is a battle. If you struggle with fear, don't beat yourself up for it--God doesn't. Just allow God to change your thinking by His Spirit living in you. Keep meditating on and praying the Love Prayer. God wants to answer it for you. Your walk with the Father will never be the same. God bless you!

Much love,

Marci Julin ☺

Verses for Meditation:

Let those who fear the LORD say, 'His love endures forever.' In my anguish I cried to the LORD, and he answered by setting me free. The LORD is with me, I will not be afraid. (Psalm 117:4-6)

The Love Prayer

(personalized)

I pray that out of his glorious riches he may strengthen me with power through his Spirit in my inner being, so that Christ may dwell in my heart through faith.

And I pray that I, being rooted and established in love, may have power, together with all the saints, to grasp how wide and long and high and deep is the love of Christ, and to know this love that surpasses knowledge— that I may be filled to the measure of all the fullness of God.

Now to him who is able to do immeasurably more than all I ask or imagine, according to his power that is at work within me, to him be glory in the church and in Christ Jesus throughout all generations, forever and ever! Amen.

Ephesians 3:16-21

About the Author

Born in southern California but primarily raised in the Atlanta area, Marci Julin is one of four children. At a young age she heard the Gospel in a Baptist Sunday school class and responded by placing her trust in Jesus Christ for salvation.

While attending Bryan College, a Christian liberal arts college in Dayton, Tennessee, she met and married Seth, her husband now of over 23 years. Before the birth of their son, they moved to the Orlando, Florida area to be near family and have continued to reside there. Although she graduated from Bryan with a bachelor's degree in elementary education and a minor in Bible, Marci chose to be a homemaker and homeschool their only child, Caleb, through the 7th grade. She then taught for two years at her son's classical Christian school.

In spite of always feeling God's hand on her life and desiring to please Him, Marci struggled with depression and trusting that God loved her personally due to many years of plaguing health problems. As a type A, driven person she continued pushing herself to her physical limits, always striving to be perfect in everything in order to win the approval of her Lord. It wasn't until God allowed her to become bedridden that she was forced to deal with her misconceptions about God and His deep, unfailing love for her. As the merciful Savior brought healing to her heart and mind through Scripture, He also brought complete physical healing. She now wholeheartedly agrees with the Psalmist when he says, *It was good for me to be afflicted so that I might learn your decrees. The law from your mouth is more precious to me than thousands of pieces of silver and gold* (Psalm 119:71-72).

Marci began Heart & Mind Ministries and has devoted her time to biblical teaching, writing, and speaking. She also enjoys traveling and exploring the beautiful areas of God's amazing creation with her family, running, gardening, and studying God's Word.

Check her out on Facebook at

https://www.prod.facebook.com/marci.julin.

You can also follow her writing on her blog,

Full of Heart and Deep in Thought

https://www.heartandmindministries.com

72

About Heart & Mind Ministries

Heart and Mind Ministries was born out of a desire by Marci Julin to inspire other Christian women to love God and His Word with passion and to seek to know Him more.   Christians don't have to check their brains at the door to believe the Bible. We have a faith that stands up to the test of time, to the criticism of skeptics, and to personal scrutiny. We can and should ask difficult questions and dig deeply to study and understand the Scriptures. In addition, as women, God has created us to feel things deeply with our hearts. The women who were last at the cross and first at the tomb were motivated, not just by a knowledge of Jesus, but by an overwhelming love for Him.

God gifts each of His servants in unique ways, and Marci Julin's teaching embodies both a truly personal, and yet an intellectual approach. With a mind that seeks order and understanding Marci loves to dig deep for the treasures that abound in Scripture.   Come join Marci in the pursuit by subscribing to her website, so that you do not miss any of the free resources she offers.

https://www.heartandmindministries.com

Schedule her to speak at your next women's event.

Contact her through the ministry's website.